Relationship Builders

Ages 4-8

Relationship Builders

by
Joy Wilt
Bill Watson

Ages 4-8

WORD

EDUCATIONAL PRODUCTS DIVISION

Waco, Texas

ISBN 0–8499–8126–3

To
Mitzi and Matthew Watson
and to All the Other Children in the World
Who Will, WE HOPE, Develop
Positive Relationships with Other Children

ACKNOWLEDGMENTS

We would like to thank Terre Watson, Robert C. Harrison, and Mary Donnelly for researching and writing many creative relationship builders.

Our deep appreciation also goes to Rosanne Crist, who typed the original manuscript; Pam Thorsen and Pat Pratt, Editors; Christina Kierman, Design Editor; and Jack Woodward, who developed the photographs.

CONTENTS

INTRODUCTION

Competition is healthy and good for all individuals. Competition provides growth potential, for it presents a challenge that can be met in a short amount of time. In other words, the results are known right away, and the results are what relationship builders are all about. Competition should be fun and should involve all the participants all the time. When winning becomes one's prime objective, then competition begins to present problems. One begins to see violence, injuries, neurotic behavior, and emotional conflicts, and negative relationships develop. Professional athletes have been, are, and always will be models that most children respect and admire. Every day professional athletics become more violent, more win-oriented, and less rule-conscious. This type of competition affects children. How many times do we ask our children: Well, did you win? How did you do? What did you win? How many points did you score? How many hits did you have? Did you win? Why not ask these questions: Did you have fun? Did you learn anything? Did you help anyone? Did you meet any new boys or girls? Do you want to go back?

The purpose of this book is to introduce many varied activities that are competition oriented but emphasize cooperation, being part of a team, fun and trust. In these activities, competition is used to build self-confidence, self-awareness, and mutual trust. Rules can be adjusted to make the games more fun and the goals easier to obtain. When conducting an activity, don't hesitate to make variations. Sometimes the changes will work; sometimes they won't. But often the variations that do not work become the most fun. Also let the children make some variations; after all, they are the ones playing. Try to stay away from scorekeeping, winning, and losing. Remember: The people participating in the activity are much more important than the activity.

GAMES

1

BALLOON STUFFING

SUGGESTED NUMBER: 6 or more

MATERIALS AND SUPPLIES

1. Adult-size overalls or baggy pants and long-sleeve sweat-shirts
2. Approximately 30 balloons per group

PROCEDURE

1. Divide the children into groups, and give each group a similar set of clothes and approximately 30 balloons.
2. One child in each group puts on the baggy, oversized clothes.
3. Some members of each group begin to blow up balloons and tie them.
4. The remainder of each group begins stuffing the tied-off balloons into the clothing.
5. After each group has filled their friend to capacity, have a parade of the balloon-filled children.
6. Then have all the children select the child whose clothing is filled with the most balloons.
7. Finally, have the entire group count the number of balloons with which each child has been stuffed. If a balloon has not been blown up to capacity, it should not be counted.

VARIATION

On a hot day, use water balloons.

KID SORTING

SUGGESTED NUMBER: 10 or more

MATERIALS AND SUPPLIES: None

PROCEDURE

1. Inform the group that you are going to whisper the name of an animal to each player and that he or she is not to tell anyone.
2. Have the entire group practice the sounds of the various animals you have selected. For example, ask them what a dog sounds like.
3. The leader or a group of leaders walk around and give each youngster an animal name.
4. Participants are asked to close their eyes and begin making the sound of the animal they were given.
5. The purpose of the game is for each group of animals to come together. Participants should continue to make their animal sounds until all like animals have found one another.
6. These groups can become teams for your next activity if you wish.

VARIATIONS

1. Use any items that make distinctive noises, such as trains, cars, police cars, or fire engines.
2. Use short verses, names, or nursery rhymes to say over and over.
3. An activity such as driving, swimming, marching, or hammering could also be used.

ICE MELTING

SUGGESTED NUMBER: 4 or more

MATERIALS AND SUPPLIES

A 5-pound or 2-pound block of ice for each group

PROCEDURE

1. Give each team a block of ice.
2. The teams are to try to melt the ice without using water or chipping or crushing it.

STICK RUN

SUGGESTED NUMBER: Groups of 5

MATERIALS AND SUPPLIES

A 6-feet long, lightweight pole for each group

PROCEDURE

1. The members of each group straddle the pole and hold onto it.
2. The group runs through a designated course, competing against the clock or another group.

VARIATION

Play tag.

ROYAL COURT

SUGGESTED NUMBER: 10 or more

MATERIALS AND SUPPLIES: None

PROCEDURE

1. Participants select a person to be the queen or king bug.
2. The role of the queen or king bug is to tag other bugs (participants), who thus become part of the court.
3. If 2 or more bugs are hugging one another, they are safe and cannot be tagged.
4. Play the game until all bugs have been tagged.

CATERPILLAR WALK

SUGGESTED NUMBER: 4 or more

MATERIALS AND SUPPLIES: None

PROCEDURE

1. Divide the participants into pairs.
2. One child in each pair sits on the ground. The other sits behind him or her and locks his or her legs around the partner's waist.
3. Using the front child's feet and both children's hands, the pair moves forward.
4. When the pair is moving smoothly, the leader can suggest that the pairs hook together to form a longer caterpillar.
5. The goal is to have the entire group locked together and moving.

MUSICAL GLASSES

MATERIALS AND SUPPLIES

1. 1 pitcher of water
2. 8 glasses

PROCEDURE

1. Fill each glass with a different amount of water.
2. Tap the glasses with a spoon to determine the order in which the glasses should be placed to form a musical scale.
3. Experiment to see if you can play a tune.
4. All members should participate.

STUFF THE BLANKET

SUGGESTED NUMBER: 4 or more

MATERIALS AND SUPPLIES

1. 1 blanket
2. 1 sheet of plywood with a hole approximately 2 feet in diameter, about hip height

PROCEDURE

1. Divide the children into groups of 2 or more.
2. Lay the blanket approximately 15 feet from the piece of plywood.
3. Ask the group to pick up the blanket and stuff it through the hole *without* using their hands or arms.

Erect other obstacles that the participants must overcome before getting to the hole, such as a row of chairs through which they weave in and out, a string raised 1 foot off the ground over which they have to jump, and so on.

TEAM LEAPFROG

SUGGESTED NUMBER: 6 or more

MATERIALS AND SUPPLIES: None

PROCEDURE

1. Divide the children into equal groups of 2 or 3 participants.
2. The children in group 1 kneel on all fours—an arm's length apart, side by side—becoming frogs.
3. The other children hold hands with the members of their own group and line up directly behind one another.
4. The children in group 2, while holding hands, leap over the frogs and then kneel on all fours, becoming frogs also.
5. The children in group 3, while holding hands, leap over both groups of frogs and then also become frogs by kneeling on all fours.
6. When all children have become frogs, the first group stands, joins hands, and leaps.
7. The game continues in this manner until a specified destination has been reached.

MACHINE WORKS

SUGGESTED NUMBER: 5 to 10

MATERIALS AND SUPPLIES: None

PROCEDURE

1. Arrange the participants in a circle.
2. Give each a specific action:
   Turning with outstretched hands
   Opening and closing his or her mouth
   Jumping up and down
   Tapping his or her shoulders
   Pulling something invisible
3. A child may only do his or her action when touched by the person in front of him or her.
4. Start the machine by touching the first player.
5. When the first player touches the second, that child begins his or her action while the first child continues to do his or her own.
6. The second child touches the third, and he or she touches the fourth, beginning another action.
7. Before you know it, the machine should be in running order.
8. To stop the action, have the last child touch the first child.
9. The first child touches the second and so on until the action stops.

VARIATION

Add noises to each action.

MUSICAL CAPTURE

SUGGESTED NUMBER: 10 or more

MATERIALS AND SUPPLIES

1. Record player
2. Records
3. Room full of various objects

PROCEDURE

1. Divide the participants into pairs. Partners join hands and stand in a circle.
2. When the music starts, the group marches in a circle.
3. While the music is playing, the leader calls out the name of an object in the room.
4. When the music stops, partners—still holding hands—run and find the object.
5. Partners must hold hands when capturing an object.
6. The couple carries the object to the leader.

STRING PARTNERS

SUGGESTED NUMBER: 10 or more

MATERIALS AND SUPPLIES

1 very long string for every 2 people

PROCEDURE

1. Starting at one end and continuing across the room, run each string around the furniture (under tables, around chairs or any other obstacles).
2. Divide the group in half.
3. Send one group to where the string ends and the other to where the string begins.
4. Each member takes an end of the string and without breaking it, winds it up, following wherever it leads.
5. The object is to meet the person on the opposite end of your string.

LAUGH AND FROWN

SUGGESTED NUMBER: 12 or more

MATERIALS AND SUPPLIES: Hat

PROCEDURE

1. Divide the participants into 2 groups. Each group forms a line and faces the other group, about 5 feet apart.
2. The leader stands between them with a hat.
3. The leader explains that he or she is going to throw the hat into the air. If it lands right side up, everyone in group 1 should laugh as hard as they can while group 2 stays perfectly quiet and doesn't smile. If the hat lands wrong side up, the players in group 2 must laugh while group 1 remains silent.
4. If anyone laughs or even smiles a wide grin when he or she is supposed to be quiet, he or she is sent to the other side.

PEOPLE OBSTACLE

MATERIALS AND SUPPLIES: None

PROCEDURE

1. The participants form a single file. If there are more than 9, divide into 2 groups.
2. The first person steps forward and positions his or her body so that the next child must go under, over, or around him or her, that is, the first child forms an obstacle.
3. Each person moves forward and, after surmounting the other human obstacles, also becomes an obstacle.
4. The children should be instructed not to duplicate an obstacle.
5. After each child has become an obstacle, the first child repeats the steps.
6. The game continues until the group reaches a designated spot.
7. The following are some suggestions for obstacle forms: (1) Standing with feet spread apart—the child goes through the legs; (2) kneeling on all fours—the child crawls under; (3) kneeling on all fours—the child steps over; (4) lying flat on back or stomach—the child jumps over.

TEAM HIDE-AND-SEEK

SUGGESTED NUMBER: 10 or more

MATERIALS AND SUPPLIES: None

PROCEDURE

1. Divide the participants into two teams.
2. One team hides while the other counts to a specified number or waits for a designated signal.
3. The hiding group may hide individually or in small groups.
4. The goal of the hiding group is to return to a predetermined home base without being caught.
5. The seekers catch opponents by tagging them.
6. After all have been caught, reverse the roles.

FEATHER FLOAT

SUGGESTED NUMBER: Unlimited

MATERIALS AND SUPPLIES

1. Feather
2. Watch with second hand

PROCEDURE

1. The object of the game is to see how long the players can keep a feather in the air by blowing it.
2. Group children together tightly.
3. The leader blows the feather into the air and keeps time.
4. Before the game starts, have each player guess how long the feather will stay in the air.
5. If there are more than 10 players, divide into groups of 5 or 6.

HIDE AND SQUEEZE

SUGGESTED NUMBER: 10 or more

MATERIALS AND SUPPLIES: None

PROCEDURE

1. The participants choose 1 child to be the bear.
2. The bear hides (hibernates) while the group counts to 100.
3. Now the group sets out to find the bear.
4. When a child finds the bear, he or she hides with him or her instead of telling the group.
5. The hiding place may be changed or stay the same.
6. When everyone has found the bear, the participants select a new bear, and the game continues.

ANIMALS AND HUNTERS

SUGGESTED NUMBER: 8 or more

MATERIALS AND SUPPLIES: None

PROCEDURE

1. Divide the players into 2 equal teams. One team represents the animals; the other, the hunters.
2. Each team marks off a home base at the end of the room.
3. The animals decide which type they are (deer, bear, lion, and so on).
4. Then the animals walk across the room near the hunters' home.
5. The hunters guess what animal they are.
6. As soon as the correct animal is named, the animals turn and run for home while the hunters give chase.
7. Any animal caught before reaching home becomes a hunter.
8. The remaining animals choose a new name and try again.

BOXCAR

SUGGESTED NUMBER: 12 or more

MATERIALS AND SUPPLIES: None

PROCEDURE

1. Players divide into groups of 3. Each group (boxcar) hooks together by placing their arms around one another's waists. Then the groups form a single file.
2. Each boxcar scatters with a double goal: (1) the front of the boxcar tries to hook on to the back of another boxcar; (2) the back of the boxcar tries not to allow anyone to hook on to him or her.

DRIBBLE SCRIBBLE

SUGGESTED NUMBER: 5 or more

MATERIALS AND SUPPLIES

1. Paper for each child
2. Crayons for each child

PROCEDURE

1. The group sits on chairs forming a circle.
2. Give each child a piece of paper and crayons.
3. Instruct the children to scribble a short line of any shape— bends, zigzags, curves, and so on—on the paper.
4. Each child then passes his or her paper to the person on the left.
5. The object is for each child to draw a picture using the scribble as starting point.

BELL CHASE

SUGGESTED NUMBER: 8 or more

MATERIALS AND SUPPLIES

1. String of bells
2. Blindfolds for all but one child

PROCEDURE

1. One person is given a string of bells to be worn around his or her neck and thus becomes the bell child.
2. Give all others rolled-up newspapers and blindfold them.
3. The bell child moves about the room, dodging those who are blindfolded.
4. They try to tap the bell child.
5. If the bell child is tapped, the two exchange roles.

STATUE TAG

SUGGESTED NUMBER: 10 or more

MATERIALS AND SUPPLIES: None

PROCEDURE

1. One child is the tagger.
2. He or she demonstrates a pose that the other children must imitate to avoid being tagged.
3. When a child is tagged, he or she demonstrates a new pose.

BLANKET BLAST

MATERIALS AND SUPPLIES

1. 1 blanket
2. Assorted soft objects (balls, balloons, pillows, and so on)

PROCEDURE

1. Spread a large blanket on the ground.
2. Space the children equal distances apart around the outside edge of the blanket.
3. Ask the children to reach with palms down and pick up the blanket.
4. Stress teamwork in each of the following activities:
   a. Waves: Pull the blanket up and down vigorously.
   b. Dome: Raise the blanket overhead in unison and pull it down quickly.
   c. Objects: Put a ball in the center of the blanket. Start with the blanket low and jerk it up. Have the children see how high they can toss the ball and still be able to catch it. (Add more balls or other objects.)
   d. Ejects: By making waves, see how quickly the children can throw an object off the blanket. (Add more objects.)
   e. Half and Half: Divide the children into 2 groups. Place a ball in the center of the blanket. The purpose is to toss the object off the blanket over to the opponents' side.

BODY SQUEEZE

SUGGESTED NUMBER: 6 or more

MATERIALS AND SUPPLIES

Large balloons

PROCEDURE

1. Ask the children to blow up the balloons.
2. Give each group the same number of inflated balloons.
3. Ask the children to break the balloons by using body pressure. No hands are to be used.
3. As a group finishes, have them cheer for another group.

FIND YOUR PARTNER'S HAND

SUGGESTED NUMBER: 2 or more

MATERIALS AND SUPPLIES

Blindfolds

PROCEDURE

1. Divide the children into pairs.
2. Partners stand facing each other at arms' length.
3. Ask each pair to touch hands and then close their eyes or put on their blindfolds.
4. Drop hands and spin around 3 times.
5. Then without opening their eyes or taking off their blindfolds, each person tries to relocate his or her partner's hand.

CRACK A SMILE

SUGGESTED NUMBER: 8 or more

MATERIALS AND SUPPLIES: None

PROCEDURE

1. Form 2 teams and ask them to face each other in lines about 4 feet apart.
2. The 2 players opposite each other become challengers.
3. One at a time each set of challengers, always facing each other, attempts to make the other smile or laugh.
4. The two challengers step forward and walk to the other end of the line always facing each other.
5. Teammates may help, but no one may physically touch his or her opponent or challenger.
6. If one does smile, he or she becomes a member of the opposite team.
7. The game ends when there is only one team or when all players are tired of smiling.

PUZZLE SEARCH

SUGGESTED NUMBER: 10 or more

MATERIALS AND SUPPLIES

Polaroid camera

PROCEDURE

1. Divide the children into groups, and then take a picture of each group.
2. After the group has studied the picture, have each member cut himself or herself out of the photograph.
3. Mix all the pictures together, and then spread them out on a table.
4. Each group is to put its group picture back together.
5. It would be best for a child not to locate his or her own picture.

VARIATIONS

1. After a group has drawn or painted a mural, cut it into a puzzle.
2. Mix the puzzle pieces with another group's mural and then have each group put its mural back together.

BLINDFOLD SCAVENGER HUNT

MATERIALS AND SUPPLIES

1. Blindfold for each group
2. Items for a scavenger hunt

PROCEDURE

1. Divide the children into groups.
2. Spread the items for the scavenger hunt all over the room.
3. Give each group a list of items to locate. The lists could be similar or different.
4. Blindfold one member of each group. When the other members of the group find an item, they call their blindfolded team member over to pick it up.
5. The blindfold should be given to other team members throughout the game.

VARIATION

1. Blindfold all members of the team except 1.
2. Place similar objects in the center of each group. As an object is called out, the blindfolded people must locate the object.
3. When the object is located, it is passed around the circle. If the majority agree to the selection of the item, the 1 member not blindfolded takes the item to the leader.
4. Obviously, the person not blindfolded cannot speak at any time.

HUMAN HUNT

SUGGESTED NUMBER: 10 or more

MATERIALS AND SUPPLIES: None

PROCEDURE

1. Divide the participants into groups.
2. Seat each group in a circle.
3. The leader asks each group for a representative with the longest hair, the darkest hair, the shortest hair, the biggest feet, the biggest hands, or the shortest, the tallest, or the one with the funniest smile, ugliest face, the one that can wiggle his or her nose, and so on.
4. The leader or the entire group selects from all the representatives the one who best fits the feature.

ROBOT WALK

SUGGESTED NUMBER: 3 or more

MATERIALS AND SUPPLIES

Large cardboard boxes with peepholes cut on each side

PROCEDURE

1. Two to 4 children put 1 box over all their heads at the same time, with each child having a peephole.
2. Now play tag, a relay game, go on an obstacle walk, conduct an indoor scavenger hunt, or just walk around the block.
3. Be sure, however, that the game uses all the children inside the box to accomplish the objective.

PUFF PONG

SUGGESTED NUMBER: 10 or more

MATERIALS AND SUPPLIES

1. Ping-Pong ball
2. Plastic coffee mugs

PROCEDURE

1. The purpose is to see how many times a Ping-Pong ball can be blown into cups that are situated in an area.
2. Put a Ping-Pong ball in the center of the room, and ask everyone to begin blowing it toward one of the cups.
3. After the ball is in the cup, try to blow it to any of the other 3 cups.
4. See how many "goals" can be made in 5 minutes or whatever time limit you choose.
5. The use of hands or feet is not permitted.
6. The cups cannot be held with hands.

VARIATIONS

1. Put out 7 or 8 balls, and see how long it takes the group to blow all of them into the cups.
2. Have the group repeat the activity 3 or 4 times to see if their skill improves.

FEED THE MONKEY

SUGGESTED NUMBER: 2 or more

MATERIALS AND SUPPLIES

1. Blindfolds
2. Large paper bibs
3. 1 banana for each child

PROCEDURE

1. Divide the group into pairs.
2. Blindfold each child, and give him or her a paper bib to protect clothes.
3. Give each child a banana. At a signal, partners feed each other the banana.
4. Since half the fun is watching other couples, let 1 or 2 pairs perform at a time.

CUP RELAY

SUGGESTED NUMBER: 8 or more

MATERIALS AND SUPPLIES

1. Cup for each child
2. Bucket of water

PROCEDURE

1. One person lies down with the container resting on him or her or just holding it.
2. The purpose is to transfer water from the bucket to the container.
3. Everyone goes at one time.

41

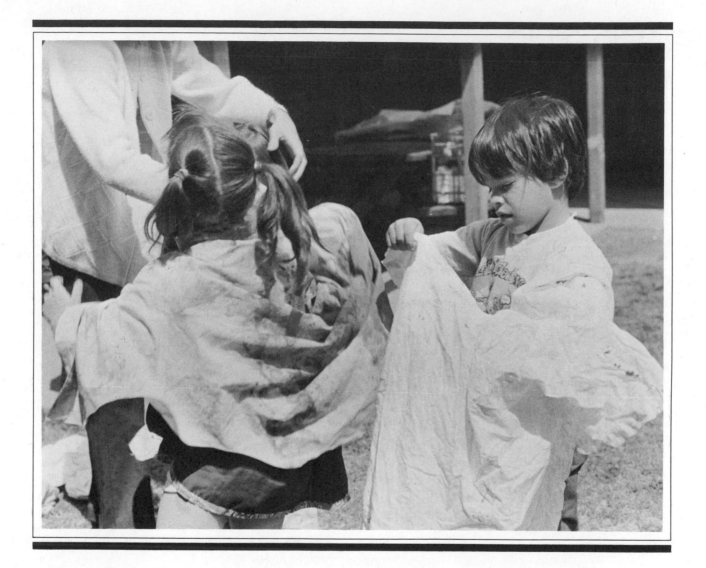

HUG-A-BUG

SUGGESTED NUMBER: 11 or more, but an odd number of participants is required.

MATERIALS AND SUPPLIES: None

PROCEDURE

1. Divide the group into pairs. Each child has a partner except 1.
2. On a given signal, everyone must find another partner by putting his or her arms around that person (front or back).

DRESSING PARTNERS

SUGGESTED NUMBER: 8 or more

MATERIALS AND SUPPLIES

For each group, similar old clothing, including hat, scarf, shirt, coat, pants, belt, shoes, socks.

PROCEDURE

1. Divide into 2 teams.
2. Each member of the team must have the clothes put on and taken off him or her.
3. Everyone on the team helps to dress and undress the others.

NEWSPAPER RACE

SUGGESTED NUMBER: 4 or more

MATERIALS AND SUPPLIES

2 newspapers for every 2 participants

PROCEDURE

1. Divide the group into pairs.
2. Designate one partner the walker; the other, the setter.
3. The walker can only walk if he or she is stepping on a newspaper.
4. The setter sets a newspaper forward, and the walker steps on it. The setter then moves the other newspaper forward in order for the walker to keep moving.
5. When a designated spot is reached, the walker and the setter reverse roles and walk back.
6. The pairs can race against one another or against the clock.

LAUGHING PICTURES

SUGGESTED NUMBER: 2 or more

MATERIALS AND SUPPLIES

A large picture frame

PROCEDURE

1. One child stands behind the picture frame.
2. The other children make funny faces or comments, trying to make the person laugh or smile.
3. Use a timer to see how long it takes to make each child laugh or smile.

WILD TUB RIDES

SUGGESTED NUMBER: 6 or more

MATERIALS AND SUPPLIES

1. 1 tub
2. 1 blanket

PROCEDURE

1. Set the tub on a blanket to prevent scratching the floor.
2. One person sits in the tub.
3. The others gather around the tub and push it through a designated course.
4. After the course is completed, another child gets to ride the wild tub.
5. The rides continue until each child has a turn.
6. Keep time for group competition.

SIMULATIONS

2

WHEN I GROW UP I WANT TO BE . . .

MATERIALS AND SUPPLIES

Paper and a pencil for each child.

PROCEDURE

1. Ask each child to list 5 people that he or she most admires.
2. Then, next to each name have the children give a reason for admiring that person. Possible answers: He or she is nice, brave, friendly, handsome, buys me things, and so on.
3. Ask the children then to make a list of the named attributes that apply to themselves.
4. Ask them also to list 2 or 3 attributes they would like to have.
5. Finally, ask them to list 2 or 3 specific things they could do during the week to develop those qualities.
6. Allow volunteers to discuss their lists.
7. Ask each child to make a self-contract on an attribute he or she will try to develop the following week.

WHAT DO YOU SEE

SUGGESTED NUMBER: 1 or more

MATERIALS AND SUPPLIES

Pictures from newspapers, magazines, party or group photographs.

PROCEDURE

Ask the children to describe and discuss what they see happening in the picture.

VARIATION

After the discussion, read the true story of the pictures, if there is one.

HOW WOULD YOU ACT?

SUGGESTED NUMBER: 1 or more

MATERIALS AND SUPPLIES

Newspaper articles about situations that might involve children.

PROCEDURE

1. Read the article to the children.
2. If it is a large group, divide into several smaller groups.
3. Ask the children how they would feel in the situation or how they would handle the situation.

GET ANGRY ABOUT

SUGGESTED NUMBER: 1 or more

MATERIALS AND SUPPLIES

Pencil and paper for each child

PROCEDURE

1. Ask each child to list all the things that make him or her angry.
2. Ask each child to select the 5 or 10 top items that make him or her angry.
3. Ask for volunteers to name one of their angers and to talk about handling that anger.
4. Other children will probably have similar angers. The discussion will show how common the angers are.

INDIVIDUAL NEEDS

SUGGESTED NUMBER: 1 or more

MATERIALS AND SUPPLIES

1. Paper and pencil for each child
2. Blackboard and chalk

PROCEDURE

1. Ask the children to think of things they do during the week, such as walk, sleep, eat, watch TV, talk, go to school, go to church, argue, play, pray, and so on.
2. Ask the group to combine their ideas and then list them on the blackboard.
3. Using the items on the blackboard as a guideline, ask each child to list the 10 items most important to him or her.
4. Have volunteers discuss their top 3 or 4 answers and explain.
5. There are no right or wrong answers.

WHAT I CAN DO WITHOUT

MATERIALS AND SUPPLIES

Paper and pencil for each child.

PROCEDURE

1. Ask each child to select from the top 10 items of his or her "Individual Needs" list the one thing he or she could do without.
2. Ask each child to try to do without that item during the following week.
3. At the next meeting talk about what each did without.
4. Questions:
   a. Was it difficult to do without that particular item?
   b. Was each child able to go through the whole week without the item?
   c. How did those who failed feel?
   d. Would the group forgive them for failing?
   e. Does the group understand why that person failed?

VARIATION

Form the children into small groups, and have each group act out the problems that occurred during the week.

LET'S HAVE A BIRTHDAY PARTY

The next 6 activities can be used as simulations in the following ways: (1) Act out the situation; (2) make up a story and change the ending; (3) read the situation to the children and discuss the questions. Change the situations and add more specifics to stimulate the children's interests.

SUGGESTED NUMBER: 1 or more

MATERIALS AND SUPPLIES: None

PROCEDURE

1. The purpose of this simulation is to show children how important their thoughts are.
2. As a group the children are to plan a birthday party.
   a. What day shall we have the party?
   b. What time of day?
   c. Where?
   d. Whom shall we invite?
   e. What kind of decorations shall we use?
   f. What kind of games shall we play?
   g. What kind of party favors shall we have?
   h. Select the food.
3. Prepare questions similar to these prior to meeting with the children.
4. Divide the children into workable groups, approximately 5 or 7.
5. Ask the group or groups to report back on their plans and how they feel about their party.
6. How would they feel if their parents had planned this party for them?

HOW I
SEE THINGS

SUGGESTED NUMBER: 10 or more

MATERIALS AND SUPPLIES: None

PROCEDURE

1. The purpose is to show children that everyone is different and thinks differently and that it is important for everyone to think for himself.
2. Children raise both hands for yes, 1 hand for no, and none if they are undecided.
3. Read aloud questions, similar to the following, beginning each with "How many of you."

   a. Would like to live on a farm?
   b. Like strawberry ice cream?
   c. Like to go to the mountains?
   d. Have a pet?
   e. Like spinach?
   f. Wish you could stay up later at night?
   g. Have a sister?
   h. Daydream?
   i. Have been to the movies in the past 2 weeks?
   j. Like to be teased?
   k. Like to tease?
   l. Know how to swim?
   m. Think boys should be allowed to play with dolls?
   n. Receive an allowance?
   o. Watch "Wonder Woman"?
   p. Are afraid of earthquakes?
   q. Have a friend in another country?
   r. Would like to change your first name?
   s. Are members of some kind of troop?
   t. Like to go to the park?

BUT I DIDN'T DO IT

MATERIALS AND SUPPLIES

Building blocks or any materials that can be stacked

PROCEDURE

1. The purpose of this simulation is to show children how to deal with anger.
2. The children act out the following situation:
   a. All the children except one, who plays the role of the mother, begin building a structure with the above materials.
   b. One child knocks the structure down, which makes the other children angry.
   c. The mother tells the children not to make so much noise and to learn to play together.
   d. Children begin rebuilding the structures.
   e. The same child knocks the structure down again, making a real mess.
   f. The other children get angry.
   g. Mother sends all the children home, makes her child clean up the mess, and tells the child to go to the bedroom.
   h. The child becomes angry.
3. Discussion
   a. What could the children do after the first time the structure was knocked down?
   b. Should they act mad at the one who knocked down the structure? How could they have handled their anger?
   c. How could the children react after the structure had been knocked down the second time?
   d. Did the child who had to clean up have a right to be angry at his or her mother?
   e. How could the anger toward the mother be handled?

PLAN A PARTY

SUGGESTED NUMBER: 5 or more

MATERIALS AND SUPPLIES

1. Shoe boxes
2. Food trays
3. Cardboard tubes
4. Colored paper or foil
5. Styrofoam
6. Small cans
7. Hard candy, popcorn peanuts, marbles
8. Tape
9. Crepe-paper strips
10. Paper plates
11. Aluminum pie plates
12. Yarn, ribbon

PROCEDURE

1. Work around a theme.
2. Give each group or person an assignment such as table decorating, favors, party hats, games, food, and so on.
3. A table decoration could be a toy that matches the theme or something made out of shoe boxes, food trays, or cardboard tubes covered with colored paper or foil. Styrofoam is a good base in which to anchor the items.
4. To make favors and/or noisemakers, fill small cans (such as empty juice cans or toilet paper tubes) with hard candy, popcorn, peanuts, pennies, marbles, and so on and seal the ends with tape and construction paper.
5. Wrap individual prizes with crepe-paper strips. Masking tape shaped into a ball or square can also be decorated.
6. Party hats can be made from paper plates, food trays, aluminum pie-plates, or cardboard squares by making a slit or hole on each side and tying a string or ribbon through the holes. They could be decorated with construction paper, foil, ribbon, yarn and so on.
7. Select food that can be decorated to reflect the theme. (See group cooking experiences, pp. 67–87.)

IF

SUGGESTED NUMBER: 1 or more

MATERIALS AND SUPPLIES: None

PROCEDURE

1. Write the "if" statements on a blackboard, and have the children write or give orally the completions.
2. Suggested "if" statements:
   a. If I did not have to go to school
   b. If I had $10.00
   c. If I could go where I wanted
   d. If I could be someone else
   e. If I were a girl/boy

WHO I THINK I AM

SUGGESTED NUMBER: 1 or more

MATERIALS AND SUPPLIES

1. Scissors
2. Old magazines
3. Glue
4. Tape
5. Construction paper

PROCEDURE

1. Each child makes a collage of himself or herself by cutting out pictures or words from the magazines.
2. Ask for volunteers to share their collages.
3. Discuss how unique each individual is.

VARIATIONS

Collages could also complete statements such as: I love to, I watch, I want to go to, or Sometimes I feel.

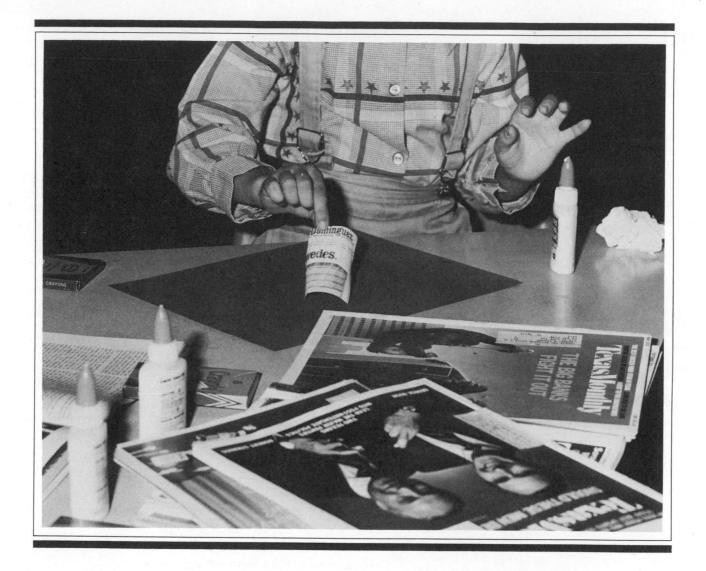

I LOOK LIKE THAT?

SUGGESTED NUMBER: 5 or more

MATERIALS AND SUPPLIES

1. Old magazines
2. Paper
3. Scissors
4. Glue

PROCEDURE

1. Divide into small groups of 5 or 6.
2. Write each individual's name on a small piece of paper and fold.
3. Each person draws another person's name.
4. The children cut out pictures, ads, or words that remind them of the person whose name they have drawn.
5. Glue the pictures and/or words on a piece of paper.
6. Looking at the collages, the children try to identify the person represented.

MY FAMILY IS DIFFERENT FROM YOURS

The following simulation activities may be used as the basis for discussion, story development, and/or play creation.

SITUATION

The purpose of this simulation is to show that everyone is put in different situations and that all these situations have good and bad points.

DISCUSSION

Ask the children questions such as:
1. How many brothers and sisters in your family?
2. Why is it good to have an older brother and/or sister, or is it?
3. Why do you wish you had an older brother and/or sister?
4. Is it good or bad to have 4 or 5 children in one family? Why?
5. Is it good or bad to be an only child? Why?
6. Is it good or bad to be the youngest or the oldest? Why?
7. How many of you have someone living with you other than your brothers, sisters, and parents?
8. How many of you have your own bedroom? Is this good and/or bad? Why?

LET'S START A CLUB

SITUATION

The group organizes a club.

DISCUSSION

1. Whose house has a large garage or extra room where the meetings can be held?
2. Whose mother could help transport children?
3. Who has some extra lumber at home to build a cupboard or storage or seats or whatever?

4. Who shall be president, vice-president, secretary, treasurer, in charge of refreshments, in charge of special trips, and so on?
5. Whose mother or father would attend most of the meetings?
6. Who will be members to help all the officers?
7. Make sure all the children play a part in the club. Point out how important each individual is and how the club would be very different if one person did not do his or her assignment or dropped out of the club.

FEELING ASHAMED

SITUATION

1. The teacher calls on a student to answer a relatively easy question.
2. The student gives the wrong answer.
3. The other children begin to laugh.

DISCUSSION

1. How would you feel if you answered the question incorrectly?
2. Doesn't everyone make mistakes?
3. Shouldn't we accept the fact that none of us is perfect?
4. Did they laugh at the student or at the answer?
5. Haven't we all been in embarrassing or uncomfortable situations? If yes, then why do we laugh at other people's mistakes?

RIGHTS AND RESPONSI- BILITY

SITUATION

1. Mother takes her child to the store to buy a pair of tennis shoes.
2. The mother sees a pair of tennis shoes she wants her child to have, but the child does not like them.
3. The child sees the pair of tennis shoes he or she wants, but the mother does not like them.

DISCUSSION

1. Which pair of shoes should be purchased?
2. Should mother select the shoes, since she knows best about shoes?
3. Should the child select the shoes, since he has to wear them?
4. If the child selects the shoes and they are not right for one reason or another (except size or manufacturer's error), should another pair of shoes be bought to replace the child's selection?

FEELING UNLOVED

SITUATION

1. A child goes to the store with his or her mother.
2. While the mother is shopping, the child looks at the toys and finds a game that a friend has, which the child enjoys very much.
3. The child finds the mother, shows the game to her, and asks her to buy it.
4. The mother says no.

DISCUSSION

1. Has this situation ever happened to you?
2. How did you feel? Do you still feel that way?
3. If this has not happened to you, how would you feel if it did?
4. How would you react toward your mother? Would that be fair?
5. Should your mother or father always buy you what you want? Why? Why not?
6. If your parents say no to your request, are they also saying they do not love you?

FEELING LONELY AND/OR DIS-APPOINTED

SITUATION

1. A child is waiting for a friend to come over and play.
2. The child has taken out some of his or her favorite games and toys and is setting them up.
3. Mother has made cookies for the occasion.
4. The friend calls and says that he or she cannot come over.

DISCUSSION

1. How would you feel if this happened to you?
2. What would you do?
3. If you started playing with your toys or games by yourself, would you still be disappointed or lonely?
4. Can you have fun by yourself?
5. Does it feel good to be by yourself sometimes? Why?

FEELING BAD

SITUATION

1. Parents are not at home.
2. Child or children are with the babysitter.
3. While playing, mother's favorite flowerpot accidentally gets knocked on the floor and is broken.

DISCUSSION

1. Whose fault is it that the pot was broken?
2. Is someone always at fault?
3. What should you do after the flowerpot is broken?
4. What should you tell your mother?
5. If you do something wrong, like breaking the flowerpot, does that make you bad?
6. Does everyone make mistakes?

FEELING LEFT OUT

SITUATION

1. Two friends are invited to a party.
2. They call you to find out if you are going, and you tell them you were not invited.

DISCUSSION

1. How would you explain to your friends that you were not going?
2. After talking to your friends, how would you feel? What would you do?

3. Was the person having the party wrong not to invite you?
4. What are some reasons you were not invited?
5. Are there people you would not invite to your party?
6. Why would you not invite them?
7. Is it necessary to like everyone you know?

NEW IN CLASS

SITUATION

1. You have just moved to a new school, and you don't know anyone.
2. You wear glasses and are kind of fat.
3. The first day, no one talks to you except your teacher.
4. The second day, the other children make fun of you for wearing glasses and being fat.

DISCUSSION

1. How would you handle this situation?
2. If you were the new person, what could you do or say to make the other children like you?
3. What kind of things could you do to help a new person?
4. Have you ever been in a situation like this? How did you feel? Did you try to help the new person?

COOKING
EXPERIENCES

3

SCRATCH-BOARD COOKIES

INGREDIENTS

4 ounces semisweet chocolate
2 tablespoons butter
   large vanilla wafers or graham crackers
   marshmallow topping

PROCEDURE

Melt the chocolate and butter in a double boiler. If the chocolate is overheated, it will become grainy and separate from the butter. Have the children spread the marshmallow topping on the cookies as evenly as possible, using a knife. Let the cookies stand a few minutes; the topping will become smooth and shiny. Have the children paint the melted chocolate on the marshmallow topping with a pastry brush, making as few brush strokes as possible. As the children continue coating the cookies, keep the chocolate mixture over hot water so that it remains thin enough to spread. Place the coated cookies on a cookie sheet and refrigerate until the chocolate is firm.

Have the children use a clean nail, skewer, or knife to scratch pictures on the cookies. The cookies are ready to be viewed and eaten.

JUNGLE JUICE

INGREDIENTS

Assortment of fresh or canned juices, including:
- grapefruit juice
- lemonade
- orange juice
- apricot nectar
- peach nectar
- apple juice
- pineapple juice

PROCEDURE

Allow each child to choose a juice and pour ½ cup of it into a large pitcher. A unique blend of jungle juice will be created.

PLAYDOUGH YOU CAN EAT

INGREDIENTS

1 large jar peanut butter
1 jar honey
1 box instant powdered milk

PROCEDURE

Spoon out two large portions of peanut butter into a bowl and add three spoonfuls of honey. Add a little powdered milk. Ask the children to mix the ingredients with their hands. Continue adding the powdered milk until the dough is no longer sticky. The children can mold it into shapes, roll it out and cut it with cookie cutters, decorate it with raisins or nuts, and—best of all—eat it.

SANDWICH TRAIN

INGREDIENTS

bread
cream cheese
peanut butter
aerosol cans of cheese-
   spread
hard-boiled eggs

raisins
bananas
olives (sliced in circles)
round carrot slices
pretzel sticks
shoestring potatoes

PROCEDURE

Have the children cut the bread slices in half so that they are in rectangular shapes. Each child can spread the cream cheese or peanut butter between his or her sandwich halves. Allow the children to decorate their sandwich halves (with items from above) to resemble a car or a train. Then have the children join all their sandwiches together to make a long train. When they have finished designing the train, they can eat a piece.

DEVILED EGGS

(*serves 10*)

INGREDIENTS

10 hard-boiled eggs
 3 tablespoons mayonnaise
 2 teaspoons vinegar
    salt, pepper, and paprika

Have the children crack and peel the hard-boiled eggs. Cut the eggs in half and remove the yolk from each half. Place the yolks, mayonnaise, and vinegar in a bowl, and allow each child a turn to mash the ingredients together with a fork. Salt and pepper the yolk mixture to taste. Have the children refill the egg halves with the yolk mixture and then sprinkle the top with paprika.

COLD CEREAL

(*serves 10*)

INGREDIENTS

5	cups nuts
1	cup sunflower seeds
1	cup wheat germ
10	apples
10	bananas
2¼	cups raisins
4	tablespoons honey or brown sugar

PROCEDURE

The nuts may already be shelled and chopped or the children may do it. Have the children chop the apples and then peel and slice the bananas. Mix all ingredients together, add milk, and eat.

PEANUT BUTTER BALLS

INGREDIENTS

½ cup powdered sugar
½ cup powdered milk
 1 cup peanut butter
 1 cup crushed graham cracker crumbs or wheat germ

PROCEDURE

Mix the sugar, milk, and peanut butter together. Have the children form the dough into balls and then roll the balls in the crumbs or wheat germ.

MILKSHAKE

INGREDIENTS

milk (⅔ cup per child)
bananas (½ per child)

PROCEDURE

Have the children mash the bananas in a bowl. In a large jar, put the correct amount of milk and banana, close the lid tightly, and have each child shake the jar. Pour into a glass. Repeat the process until everyone is served. (Four mashed strawberries or 2 tablespoons chocolate syrup may replace the banana.)

PROTEIN CANDY

INGREDIENTS

1 cup raw wheat germ
1 cup sunflower seed meal
(grind whole seeds finely
or blend in a liquifier)
½ cup whole sunflower
seeds
1 cup chopped raw nuts
1 cup powdered milk
3 cups quick-cooking oat-
meal (uncooked)

1 cup ground dates
1 cup honey
1 cup carob flour
½ cup milk
½ cup softened margarine
ground nuts, grated coco-
nut, or sesame seeds

PROCEDURE

The children may need to grind the sunflower seeds into meal.
This can be done with a rolling pin. Place the honey, milk,
ground dates, and margarine in a pan to warm. This helps
these ingredients to mix better. Combine the remaining ingredients thoroughly before adding to the liquid mixture. Have
the children roll the candy into walnut-size balls and then roll
the balls in either ground nuts, grated coconut, or sesame
seeds to avoid stickiness. Store the protein candy in the
refrigerator.

LEMONADE

INGREDIENTS

lemons
water
sugar or honey

PROCEDURE

Have the children roll the lemons on the table. This allows more juice to be obtained from the fruit. Cut the lemons in half. Using a juicer, have the children squeeze the lemon juice into a pitcher. For every ½ lemon used, add ½ cup water and 2 teaspoons sugar or honey.

CANDIED CARROTS

INGREDIENTS

1 bunch carrots
2 tablespoons brown sugar
2 tablespoons butter

PROCEDURE

Have the children scrub or peel the carrots. Remove the tops and cut carrots into slices or 2-inch sticks. Cook in a covered pan with enough salt water to cover the carrots. Depending on the size and shape of the carrots, the cooking time may vary from 10 to 20 minutes. Drain the carrots.

In a small saucepan, melt the butter and brown sugar, and heat for 3 minutes. Pour this mixture over the carrots; toss and serve.

MERINGUE

(*serves 12*)

INGREDIENTS

4 egg whites
4 tablespoons sugar
  salt

PROCEDURE

Separate the egg yolks from the egg whites. With an egg beater, have the children beat the egg whites and a dash of salt until foamy. Add the sugar slowly, and allow each child a chance to beat the egg whites until stiff peaks form. The meringue can be used to top cakes, puddings, cookies, graham crackers, or fruit.

CHRISTMAS TREE

(*serves 12*)

INGREDIENTS

 3 cups powdered sugar
 2 cups beaten egg whites (approximately 3 eggs)
 3 teaspoons soft shortening
12 pointed ice-cream cones
  popped popcorn
  raisins
  cookie decorations
  green food-coloring

PROCEDURE

Have the children take turns beating the egg whites. Mix the sugar, egg whites, soft shortening, and 3 drops green food-coloring. If the mixture is too thick, add a little water. Have the children spread the icing on the ice-cream cones. (Turn the cones upside down to resemble a tree.) Have the children decorate the trees with the popcorn, raisins, and cookie decorations.

FRUIT CREATIONS

INGREDIENTS

Assorted canned or fresh fruits:

peach halves	tangerine or orange sections
apricot halves	grated coconut
pear halves	raisins
cherries	pineapple rings
bananas	cake-decorating gel

PROCEDURE

Have the children use the various pieces of fruit to create animals, people, or faces. Here are a few examples: a lion made from a peach half on top of a pineapple ring; a mouse made with a peach half and apricot halves for ears; a monkey made with a pear half and apricot halves for ears. These may also be placed in a dish of jello. After the animals have been created, they are ready to eat.

TOSSED SALAD

INGREDIENTS

lettuce
tomatoes
cucumbers
celery
salad dressing

PROCEDURE

Have the children wash the vegetables. Tear the lettuce and place it in a bowl. The children can slice the cucumbers, tomatoes, and celery. Pour a salad dressing on top and toss.

PEANUT BUTTER

INGREDIENTS

1 pound bag of peanuts in the shell
cooking oil
peanut grinder and bowl

PROCEDURE

Have all the children shell the peanuts, leaving the brown skin on the peanut. Place the peanuts in a grinder, and let the children take turns grinding the peanuts into a bowl. Add enough oil to make the peanut butter spreadable. Serve on bread or crackers.

CHEESE AND PEANUT BUTTER STUFFING

INGREDIENTS

cheesespread
peanut butter
lettuce
celery

PROCEDURE

Have the children wash the celery and lettuce. Spread the peanut butter or cheesespread on some lettuce and roll it up. Spread the cheesespread or peanut butter in the celery.

VEGETABLE DIPPERS

INGREDIENTS

Assorted raw vegetables:
- carrots
- celery
- cucumbers
- zucchini
- cherry tomatoes
- cauliflower
- sour cream, cottage chesse, or mayonnaise base dip

PROCEDURE

Have the children wash the vegetables. Peel the carrots and cucumbers, if desired. Cut the flowers from the cauliflower. Slice the carrots, zucchini, and cucumbers into thick rounds. Slice the celery into 3-inch lengths. Place the vegetables on a tray. The vegetables can be dipped into a sour cream, cottage cheese, or mayonnaise base dip.

FRESH FRUIT SALAD

INGREDIENTS

- apples
- bananas
- pears
- tangerines
- coconut (shredded)
- ¼ cup orange juice
- 16 ounces sour cream
- 3 tablespoons honey

Have the children peel and cut up the fruits and then place them in a bowl. Combine the sour cream, honey, and orange juice and pour on top of the fruit. Toss the fruit salad, and it is ready to eat.

GRAPEFRUIT JUICE

INGREDIENTS

grapefruits
water

PROCEDURE

Have the children roll the grapefruits on the table. Cut the grapefruits in half and squeeze out the juice. For every half grapefruit used, add ½ cup water.

ORANGE JUICE

INGREDIENTS

oranges
water

PROCEDURE

Have the children roll the oranges on the table. Cut the oranges in half and squeeze the juice into a pitcher. For every half orange used, add ½ cup water.

BUTTER

INGREDIENTS

1 cup whipping cream
   salt

PROCEDURE

Pour the whipping cream into a 16-ounce jar and secure the lid. Have each child shake the jar 10 times and then pass it on to the next child, giving everyone in the group a turn. Continue shaking the jar until a ball of butter appears. Pour off the buttermilk (which is good to drink), and squeeze out the remaining buttermilk by pressing the butter against the side of the jar with a spoon. This butter will be sweet, but by adding a dash of salt, it will become salty. Spread the butter on crackers or bread and enjoy it.

WHIPPED CREAM

INGREDIENTS

1 cup whipping cream
2 tablespoons sugar

PROCEDURE

Have each child take a turn beating the whipping cream with an egg beater until it is thick. Add the sugar and continue beating until peaks appear. The whipped cream can be used to top cakes, puddings, fruits, or cookies.

HOT DOG SHISH KEBABS

INGREDIENTS

1 wiener for each child
1 large can pineapple chunks
   cherry tomatoes
   carrots
   onion
   bellpepper
   teriyaki or barbecue sauce

PROCEDURE

Have the children cut the wieners into 4 parts. All the vegetables, except the tomatoes, should be cut into chunks. The children should place one piece of wiener on the skewer, followed by a vegetable, a piece of wiener, a chunk of pineapple, another vegetable, and one more piece of wiener. End with a piece of pineapple. Spread the hot dog shish kebabs with teriyaki or barbecue sauce, and arrange them on a flat pan. Place the pan under a broiler until the meat is browned and the vegetables are tender. Hot dog shish kebabs could also be cooked outside on a grill.

VEGETABLE SOUP

INGREDIENTS

1 18-ounce can tomato juice
4 teaspoons salt
2 teaspoons worcestershire sauce
¼ teaspoon chili powder
2 bay leaves
carrots
onions

celery
bellpeppers
potatoes
corn
string beans
tomatoes
beans

PROCEDURE

The children may each bring a fresh or canned vegetable from home, or the teacher may collect the vegetables. Combine the first 5 ingredients to make the soup broth. Have the children clean, peel, slice, or cut the vegetables and place them in the broth. Cook the soup over a high heat, bringing it to a boil; then reduce the heat to simmer for half an hour. The vegetables might be a little crunchy.

APPLES ON TOAST

INGREDIENTS

apples
bread
butter
sugar
cinnamon

PROCEDURE

Preheat the oven to 375 degrees. Have the children peel and slice the apples, butter the bread, and place the apple slices on the bread. Combine 4 tablespoons sugar with 2 tablespoons cinnamon, and have the children sprinkle the mixture over the apples. Place each piece of bread on a cookie sheet and bake for 15 minutes.

PUT A FACE ON A SANDWICH

INGREDIENTS

1 loaf bread or 1 package graham crackers
1 package cream cheese, 1 jar peanut butter, 1 stick butter, or
   1 package cheese spread
1 can olives, sliced in circles
1 box raisins
1 jar cherries, sliced in different shapes
1 package chocolate chips, red hots, or gumdrops
1 package grated coconut
   grated carrots
   parsley
   sunflower seeds
   sesame seeds
   alfalfa or bean sprouts

PROCEDURE

Have the children spread the cream cheese, peanut butter, butter, or cheese spread on the crackers or bread. The children can use their imagination to make faces on their sandwiches with the other items listed. After the sandwiches have been decorated, they are ready to eat.

DIPPED BANANAS

INGREDIENTS

bananas
chocolate sauce or marshmallow cream
Granola, wheat germ, graham cracker crumbs, or Grapenuts

PROCEDURE

Have the children peel the bananas and cut them into thirds. The children can roll or dip the bananas in the chocolate sauce or marshmallow cream. Then roll the covered bananas in the Granola, wheat germ, graham cracker crumbs, or Grapenuts.

BOLOGNA AND CHEESE ROLLS

INGREDIENTS

1 large package bologna
1 large package cheese or 1 jar cheese spread

PROCEDURE

Have the children top a slice of bologna with either a slice of cheese or the cheese spread and roll it up.

DRAMA AND STORYTELLING

4

SCRAMBLE A RHYME

MATERIALS AND SUPPLIES

1. Fractured rhymes
2. Tape

PROCEDURE

1. Print a nursery rhyme on construction paper. Cut it up into 2- or 3-word segments.
2. Hide the pieces of the rhyme.
3. Ask the children to find all the pieces and put them together in proper order.
4. Sit back and watch the fun while they tape the rhyme together.

VARIATION

1. Cut up 2 separate nursery rhymes and mix them up.
2. Create 2 groups.
3. Give each group half the word segments.
4. Tell the group they must bargain and trade to complete their rhyme.
5. Tape the rhymes together and mount in the classroom.

MAKING BUTTERFLIES

SUGGESTED NUMBER: 5 to 15

MATERIALS AND SUPPLIES

Imagination

PROCEDURE

1. Talk with your group about butterflies. What colors have you seen? How high do they fly? How do they become butterflies? (Start as an egg, then become a caterpillar, form a cocoon, and finally emerge as a butterfly.)
2. Ask the children to make themselves into tiny eggs.
3. When it is time to hatch, they turn into caterpillars. Ask, "Can you crawl like a caterpillar?"
4. Pretty soon the caterpillar builds a special house for himself. It is called a cocoon. He puts lots of special thread around himself. "Can you make a cocoon?"
5. A cocoon is a good place for sleeping. You must be very still while in a cocoon.
6. While the caterpillar is sleeping, something special happens. He becomes a butterfly.
7. Can you come out of your cocoon? What beautiful butterflies! Can you fly?
8. Let your butterflies fly around the room.
9. Talk about how it feels to be a caterpillar asleep in a cocoon and a butterfly flying around.

MAKING VEGETABLE SOUP

MATERIALS AND SUPPLIES

1. Imaginary stove
2. Imaginary pots and spoons
3. Imaginary vegetables

PROCEDURE

1. Talk with your children about all the things that go into making vegetable soup—carrots, peas, onions, beans, potatoes, and so on.
2. With the group pick all the imaginary vegetables from their imaginary vines. Remember how these grow when you are picking them. Carrots and potatoes grow underground, but peas grow on a vine.
3. Put all the vegetables in different piles. Talk about their color, weight, and smell.
4. Give each child some of each vegetable.
5. Prepare each vegetable for cooking: Peel the potatoes, cut the greens off the carrots, shell the peas, peel the onions (don't forget how they make you cry).
6. Give each child an imaginary knife and cutting board. Tell them to be sure to keep the sharp edges away from their fingers.
7. Chop all the vegetables into little pieces.
8. Put all the vegetables in an imaginary pot and add a little water. Talk about how heavy the pot is. Let each child lift the pot.
9. Turn on the imaginary stove and cook the vegetable soup. Give each child a turn to stir.
10. When each child has had a turn, turn off the stove and dish out the soup.
11. Enjoy a delicious meal.

GROW A HUMAN GARDEN

MATERIALS AND SUPPLIES

Floor space

PROCEDURE

1. Before growing your own classroom garden, talk with the group about flower seeds. What do they need to grow? (Soil, sun, water, time)
2. Tell the children that they are going to be seeds.
3. Have them dig a big imaginary hole for themselves.
4. Ask them to make themselves as small as a tiny seed.
5. Now instruct them to put themselves in the holes they just dug.
6. You as the gardener will be in charge of the rest of their cultivation.
7. Put extra dirt on top of the seeds, gently patting each child on the back.
8. Next the seeds need some rain; so tap each child on the head. Ask questions such as the following: Are you plants thirsty? Does the water taste good?
9. The sunshine is the next ingredient needed for growth; so provide sunshine by rubbing their backs. Ask the children if they can feel the sunshine. Is it warm?
10. Encourage your young blooms to grow: "My! Some of my flowers are already growing. I hope the rest bloom soon."
11. Before you know it, you'll have a classroom garden of smiles.
12. You can follow up by asking questions such as these: What kind of plant are you? What color are your flowers? Do you like being a plant?
13. Tend your human plants carefully.

CREATE A POEM

MATERIALS AND SUPPLIES

1. Paper
2. Pencils

PROCEDURE

1. Each child will have a turn to write a line of poetry.
2. Ask the first child to write 1 line.
3. The child then folds the paper so that the line cannot be seen.
4. The child then whispers the last word of his or her line to the next child and passes the paper to him or her.
5. The next child writes another line to rhyme with the first child's last word.
6. This continues until everyone has had a turn.
7. Read the poem aloud.

ART CHARADES

SUGGESTED NUMBER: 5 to 15

MATERIALS AND SUPPLIES

1. Crayons
2. Paper
3. Prepared charade phrases
4. Young imagination

PROCEDURE

1. Write phrases, sentences, or names of objects on slips of paper. These could include nursery rhymes, TV programs, or animals.
2. Give the child who will be doing the charade a piece of paper, some crayons, and a charade sentence.
3. The child is to express his or her phrase without the use of words and by using crayon art work. You may want to tape the paper up high so the group can see it.
4. The children in the group try to guess the charade. When a child guesses the correct charade, he or she goes up and tries his or her hand at art charades. The children may keep their art work.

VARIATIONS

1. Use paint instead of crayons.
2. Use chalk to draw the charade expressions on the sidewalk. (It will wash off.)
3. Use finger paints.
4. If you find yourself outside, draw the pictures in wet sand or dirt.
5. To involve the group more extensively, do group art charades. You could use a well-known theme or story.
    a. Prepare charade slips using only part of a well-known story. Phrases could include "And I'll huff and I'll puff" or "This one made his house of straw."
    b. Each child would be given one phrase to draw.
    c. As each phrase is guessed, the picture could be mounted in order on a piece of paper to create a story in pictures.

REVOLVING WORDS

PROCEDURE

1. Seat your group in a circle.
2. Tell them they will be creating a story, using 5 words at a time.
3. Start the story by giving the first 5 words (Once upon a time there . . .).
4. The story passes around the circle, each child giving 5 words at a time (Once upon a time, there was a little teeny tiny . . .).
5. The story continues to build around the circle, each child adding a bit (Once upon a time, there was a little teeny tiny man with a very huge . . .). To make it more difficult, start cutting down the amount of words they can use at one time: 4, 3, 2, 1.

SAFARI TO AFRICA

SUGGESTED NUMBER: 5 to 15

MATERIALS AND SUPPLIES

Your imagination

PROCEDURE

1. Take a pretend safari with your group.
2. First, discuss what you'll need for a safari (what kind of clothes, equipment, and so on).

3. Discuss how you will get to Africa (plane, train, big bird, horses).
4. Pantomime actions to gather food and supplies, purchase tickets, and get ready for takeoff.
5. Ask your group how they like the trip over to Africa. Allow free response.
6. Once you are in Africa, begin to prepare with pantomime for the safari—change your clothes, put on your hiking boots, load your camera.
7. Talk about what you see on the safari. "Oh, look! An elephant! What do you see?" Allow free response.
8. Take a pretend walk through the jungle—push back the bushes, swat at mosquitoes.
9. Ask questions that will stimulate their imaginations. (Pick a fruit and taste it. What does it taste like? Smell a flower. What does it smell like? Touch a monkey. How does it feel?)
10. Continue your safari until nightfall when it's time to go home. Be sure to take lots of pictures. Everyone will want to see them when you get back.

VARIATIONS

1. Trip to the grocery store
2. Trip to a costume gallery
3. Trip to the zoo
4. Trip to the circus
5. Trip to the beach to go scuba diving
6. Trip to the airport
7. Trip to the ice cream parlor

STORY PASTE

SUGGESTED NUMBER: 4 or more

MATERIALS AND SUPPLIES

1. Numerous magazines
2. Posterboard
3. Glue

PROCEDURE

1. Read to the group a short story with a message.
2. Divide the main group into groups of 4.
3. By using old magazines and newspapers, the subgroups make a collage of pictures and words that best describe the story.
4. Everyone unites and describes the collages, eventually placing all collages together to form a large collage.

STORY GRAPHS

SUGGESTED NUMBER: 5 or more

MATERIALS AND SUPPLIES

Pictures from old magazines

PROCEDURE

1. Divide into small groups. Each group takes 7 or 8 pictures and invents a story.
2. Each group then gives its presentation to the entire group.
3. Each member of the group should verbally participate.
4. The pictures can be held up or glued on butcher paper and presented in a scroll manner.

1. Have children draw their own pictures.
2. Use an overhead projector.
3. Combine the pictures with the children's drawings.

AUDIO TALES

SUGGESTED NUMBER: 5 or more

MATERIALS AND SUPPLIES

1. Tape recorder for each group and microphones for recording
2. Blank tapes

PROCEDURE

1. Each group is given 5 related nouns or a bag of clothing or a nursery rhyme. Each group is to make up a story using what it has been given.
2. Tape the story of each group, and play all tapes for the entire group.
3. If you run out of time, use the tapes for your next meeting.

SHADOW PLAY

MATERIALS AND SUPPLIES

1. White sheet
2. Strong lamp

PROCEDURE

1. Hang a sheet in front of the lamp.
2. Turn off all other lights.
3. Have the children put on a play or other dramatic activity behind the sheet.

TAPE LISTENING

SUGGESTED NUMBER: 4 or more

MATERIALS AND SUPPLIES

Tape recorder

PROCEDURE

1. Have the children individually talk into a tape recorder and play it back.
2. Divide into groups and have each member of the group talk into the tape recorder.
3. After everyone has been taped, play it back, and have the children guess who was speaking.

PICTURE POSE

SUGGESTED NUMBER: Unlimited

MATERIALS AND SUPPLIES

Photographs of people

PROCEDURE

1. Divide the children into groups, corresponding to the number of people in the pictures.
2. Assign each group a picture and give the members a few minutes to pick a character in the photo to portray in a short skit.
3. The performing group takes the exact position of the pictured characters.
4. On the command of "Action," each group performs its skit until the command of "Cut."

BRAIN-STORMING

SUGGESTED NUMBER: 2 or more

MATERIALS AND SUPPLIES

Nursery rhymes

PROCEDURE

1. Read a nursery rhyme, omitting key words.
2. Without letting the group know the rhyme, ask them to supply the missing words by telling them the type of word needed (a color, number, part of the body, exclamation, and so on.)
3. Encourage the group to be as imaginative as possible.
4. After all blanks have been filled, read back the nursery rhyme.

STORY WEAVING

SUGGESTED NUMBER: 10 or more

MATERIALS AND SUPPLIES

Ball of yarn

PROCEDURE

1. The group invents a story, each person saying only 1 word or phrase.
2. As each child finishes a portion, he or she, holding onto the yarn, throws the ball of yarn to another person.
3. After the story has been completed, with all children adding to the story, notice the weaving that has been created.
4. Emphasize that only through total participation could the story and the weaving have been created.
5. Have one child after another let go of his or her end of the yarn. Emphasize that as 1 or 2 individuals stop contributing, the weaving, or the group, begins to fall apart.

VARIATION

This is a good introduction activity. Instead of telling a story, each child gives his or her name.

HOW DO YOUR FEET FEEL?

SUGGESTED NUMBER: 5 to 15

MATERIALS AND SUPPLIES

Feet

PROCEDURE

1. Introduce this activity by talking about the children's feelings. How do they feel when they are angry, happy, or sad?
2. Ask the children to let their feet speak for their feelings. Their feet can tell the story of how they feel.
3. Ask the children, How do you feel when you are happy? Maybe their feet would dance or run or maybe just their toes would wiggle. Ask, how do you feel when you are angry? Perhaps they would stomp their feet.
4. Go on to more specific questions. How would you feel if you were lost in a big store? How would you feel if you had just found a dollar?
5. Remind the children that they cannot use their feet on someone else. For example, if they are acting angry, they may not kick someone.

VARIATIONS

1. Ask the children to take off their shoes.
2. Have the children sit on the floor. Put a blanket on their legs so only their feet show. This will emphasize that only the feet do the acting.

RIDING ON A CLOUD

SUGGESTED NUMBER: 5 to 10

MATERIALS AND SUPPLIES

Imagination

PROCEDURE

1. Talk to the children about clouds. What do they look like? Are they fluffy? Pretend to pick one up. Is it heavy or light? If possible, go outside to look at some clouds.
2. Get your imaginary cloud-nets out. Sneak up on a low-lying cloud and catch it in your net.
3. Take out your imaginary rope. Tie it up so that it doesn't float away.
4. Go get your cloud saddles. They are a lot like horse saddles but very, very light.
5. Put the saddle on the cloud you caught, and get ready for your trip.
6. Let your cloud take you anywhere it wants to go.
7. What do you see below? The people look like ants. The houses look like toys.
8. What kind of land are you flying over? Mountains? Deserts? Oceans?
9. Keep your cloud flying until you are ready to head for home.
10. Unsaddle your cloud and set it free again. Be sure to hang up your saddle.

SWIMMING INDOORS

MATERIALS AND SUPPLIES: None

PROCEDURE

1. Tell your class about the new imaginary pool for your classroom.
2. Ask the children if they would like to go swimming.
3. Be sure to put on your bathing suits!
4. First, touch the water with your big toe. Is it warm or cold?
5. Get into the water a little at a time. How does it feel when your feet are wet? How does it feel when your stomach is wet? How does it feel when your arms are wet? How does it feel when your neck is wet? How does it feel when your face is wet?
6. Swim forward, backward, underwater. Practice holding your breath. Jump into a floating ring.
7. Don't forget to dry yourself off and put dry clothes on before going back to class.

COSTUME BOX

MATERIALS AND SUPPLIES

1. Pants
2. Shirts
3. Hats
4. Coats
5. Dresses
6. Purses
7. Jewelry
8. Shoes

PROCEDURE

1. Let the children experiment with the world of dress-up.
2. Allow each child time to assemble a costume.
3. When they are comfortable with what they are wearing, put the children in groups of 2 or 3.
4. Ask them to make up a story about the kind of people that would wear those clothes.
5. Give each group a chance to act out their story before the rest of the group.
6. Don't be stingy with praise.

INDOOR PLAY-GROUND

MATERIALS AND SUPPLIES

Imagination

PROCEDURE

1. Talk with your children about some of their favorite playground activities—skipping rope, hopscotch, 4-square, swinging, catching and throwing a ball, playing jacks, climbing on monkey bars.
2. Ask each child to pantomime a particular activity.
3. When you say "go," each child pantomimes his or her activity. Who needs equipment?
4. Follow this up by having children participate together in activities such as jumping rope, having one person swing and one person pushing, one child throwing a ball and another catching it.
5. This might be good for days when it's too cold or rainy to go out to a real playground.

COULD YOU HELP ME?

SUGGESTED NUMBER: 10 to 15

MATERIALS AND SUPPLIES

Imaginary lettuce, carrots, and baby rabbits

PROCEDURE

1. Have 3 or 4 children be the carrots or the lettuce in the garden. Have them stand in a circle, holding one another tightly around the waist.
2. The other children are to be baby rabbits.
3. The first rabbit goes to the garden and tries to pick the lettuce, but it's too heavy.
4. He hops home and says to another baby rabbit, "Can you help me?" He takes the other rabbit with him back to the lettuce patch.
5. The first bunny latches on to the lettuce while the second bunny holds onto the first bunny's waist.
6. If they cannot budge the lettuce, the second bunny goes home to get a third and so on.
7. This continues until the baby bunnies can pick the lettuce.
8. When the bunnies pick the lettuce, change roles so that everyone has a turn at both characters.

TIGHTROPE WALKING

SUGGESTED NUMBER: 5 to 10

MATERIALS AND SUPPLIES

Imagination

PROCEDURE

1. Talk with your group about what a tightrope walker does. "He walks across a rope high up in the air. It could be very scary, but it might be fun."
2. Tie your imaginary tightrope up in the classroom.
3. Ask for volunteers to try the rope. Show them how to extend their arms for balance and place one foot in front of the other.
4. Tell the children that you are going to try to get all the children up on the rope.
5. One by one add each child to the group. Ask them to hold hands.
6. Now that everyone is up on the rope, try stunts such as walking forward, walking backward, jumping on the rope, hopping on the rope, and so on. Be sure to do these stunts together while holding hands.

VARIATION

Try these stunts on imaginary unicycles.

FINISH THE TALE

SUGGESTED NUMBER: 1 or more

MATERIALS AND SUPPLIES

Storybook

PROCEDURE

1. Read the first part of a story and stop.
2. Divide the children into groups.
3. Ask each group to act out the entire story with its own ending.

VARIATION

Groups could tell the entire story instead of acting it out.

CREATIVE MOVEMENTS

SUGGESTED NUMBER: 1 or more

MATERIALS AND SUPPLIES: None

PROCEDURE

Name a certain object that moves and have the children act it out. Examples: trains, cars, airplanes, animals.

VARIATION

Assign 1 child an object. As he or she is acting it out, ask the remainder of the children to identify the object.

GROUP PROJECTS

5

STAINED-GLASS WINDOW

SUGGESTED NUMBER: 5 to 10

MATERIALS AND SUPPLIES

1. Various colors of tissue paper
2. Liquid starch
3. A window in your classroom, or a plastic box
4. Scissors

PROCEDURE

1. Ask the children to cut the tissue paper into different shapes.
2. Dip the tissue paper in the starch. Squeeze out the excess between fingers.
3. Place tissue paper on glass, overlapping it in every direction.
4. Cover the entire glass this way, making sure all the tissue edges are smoothed down.
5. Let the starch dry, and your window is finished.

BALL PUPPETS

SUGGESTED NUMBER: 3 to 10

MATERIALS AND SUPPLIES

1. Crayons
2. Scrap materials:
   felt
   sequins
   yarn
3. Styrofoam balls
4. Glue
5. Scissors

PROCEDURE

1. Give each child a styrofoam ball and access to all the scrap materials.
2. With a pair of closed scissors, make a hole in the styrofoam ball. It should be deep enough to fit on the child's finger.
3. Make puppets by decorating the balls. The puppets could illustrate a story or a story could be made up about the puppets.

MURALS

A variety of activities can evolve around creating group murals. To complete a picture requires total group participation and imagination. The following 4 outlines are suggested mural concepts. You can have fun inventing your own.

MURAL NO. 1: THE FOUR SEASONS

SUGGESTED NUMBER: 12 to 25

MATERIALS AND SUPPLIES

1. 4 large pieces of butcher paper
2. Scissors
3. Glue
4. Magazines

PROCEDURE

1. Divide the group into 4 sections and give each a season— winter, spring, summer, or fall.
2. Ask the children to look through the magazines for words and pictures that remind them of their season.
3. Cut them up and glue them on the paper. Put all 4 seasons together and you have a year in pictures.

MURAL NO. 2: STRING FEELINGS

SUGGESTED NUMBER: 10

MATERIALS AND SUPPLIES

1. Glue
2. String (varied colors and textures)
3. Scissors
4. Heavy paper

PROCEDURE

1. Give the group a feeling to think about such as, "What is it like to be happy or sad?"
2. Give them glue, string, and scissors and ask them to make pictures of their feelings with string.
3. The end result, besides sticky fingers, will be a collage of young feelings.

MURAL NO. 3: STORY MURAL

SUGGESTED NUMBER: 5 to 10

MATERIALS AND SUPPLIES

1. A story or nursery rhyme
2. Crayons or paint
3. Paper

PROCEDURE

1. Tell the group a short story.
2. Assign each child a section of the story to illustrate on a large piece of paper.

MURAL NO. 4: SAND-CASTING

SUGGESTED NUMBER: 2 to 20

MATERIALS AND SUPPLIES

1. Boxes of wet sand.
2. Bucket
3. Plaster of Paris

PROCEDURE

1. Smooth out the wet sand.
2. Draw a design with your finger ¼ to ½ inch deep.
3. Mix the plaster in the bucket.
4. Carefully pour the plaster over the design, allowing it to fill all the crevices.
5. Allow the plaster to harden.
6. Remove the plaster from the stand, and you have a design.
7. Do this individually, or use a large box for the entire group to do a common design.

NEWSPAPER COSTUMES

MATERIALS AND SUPPLIES

1. Newspaper
2. Masking tape

PROCEDURE

1. Divide into groups of 3 to 5.
2. Give each group a role of tape and a stack of newspapers.
3. Ask them to make costumes for everyone in their group. This can be done by folding, pleating, crushing, and tearing the newspaper.
4. Finish with a fashion parade.

VARIATION

Use paper bags instead of newspapers.

DANCING CENTIPEDE

MATERIALS AND SUPPLIES

1. Large pieces of cardboard
2. Tempera paints or crayons
3. String
4. Hole puncher
5. Scissors
6. Fishing line
7. Buttons

PROCEDURE

1. Draw a centipede body (with no feet) about 3 feet long on a large piece of cardboard. Do this on a seam so that 2 may be cut out and still be connected at the top.
2. Punch holes on the seam about 1 inch apart.
3. Have the children draw centipede feet about 5 inches long on pieces of cardboard.
4. Cut out the feet and decorate them on both sides.
5. Punch a hole on the top of each foot and attach a piece of fishing line about 2 feet long.
6. Push this string through a hole on the centipede body.
7. Attach a button on the string so that it won't fall through the hole.

8. Attach all the feet in this way.
9. Attach a longer string to the head and tail of the centipede.
10. Tie the centipede between 2 chairs or have 2 children hold it.
11. Have each child take a button. Put on some music and watch the centipede dance.

STICK CONSTRUC-TIONS

SUGGESTED NUMBER: 2 to 10

MATERIALS AND SUPPLIES

1. Toothpicks
2. Ice cream sticks
3. Glue

PROCEDURE

1. Distribute the sticks and glue.
2. All the children need now is time to build cities, castles, monsters, and other things we have never thought of.

GROUP WEAVING

SUGGESTED NUMBER: 2 to 15

MATERIALS AND SUPPLIES

1. Large wooden frame
2. Hammer and nails
3. Heavy twine or yarn
4. Scrap yarn and twine
5. 2 dowels
6. Fork
7. Needle and thread

PROCEDURE

1. Make the weaving frame by hammering nails ½ inch apart in a straight line across the top and bottom of the frame.
2. Run heavy yarn or twine back and forth connecting it to the nails. This creates the warp.
3. With scrap yarn and twine, weave in and out of the warp.
4. Press the fibers together with a fork, making the weaving tight.
5. When weaving is complete, sew the top and bottom so that it will not unravel.
6. Remove from the frame, and mount 1 dowel at the top and 1 at the bottom. Your weaving is ready for hanging.

VARIATION

1. Use a wooden frame, chicken wire, scrap yarn, and twine.
2. Nail the chicken wire to the wood frame. Be sure to tack down all the edges.
3. Weave the yarn and twine in and out of the chicken wire.
4. When weaving is completed, hang with frame attached.

CITIES IN THE SAND

SUGGESTED NUMBER: 3 to 10

MATERIALS AND SUPPLIES

1. Wet sand
2. Cups and bowls
3. Scraps for decorating

PROCEDURE

1. Construct a city in the sand.
2. Use bowls, cups, and spoons for towers and domes.
3. Decorate the building with yarn, aluminum foil, and paper flags.
4. You might want to take a picture of this since the city itself isn't permanent.

BODY-PICTURE PUPPETS

SUGGESTED NUMBER: 2 to 100

MATERIALS AND SUPPLIES

1. Large piece of butcher paper
2. Paint
3. Crayons
4. String
5. Scissors

1. Each child needs a partner for this activity.
2. Have the children lie down on a piece of butcher paper.
3. The children take turns tracing one another's bodies with a crayon.
4. After each body is outlined, let each child paint his or her picture.
5. When the pictures are dry, cut them out.
6. Fold the arms accordian style to avoid ripping.
7. Attach string to the hands and feet.
8. With a partner, operate the puppet by moving the strings.
9. These could be used for introduction purposes or full skits.

STYROFOAM CONSTRUC-TION

SUGGESTED NUMBER: 2 to 10

MATERIALS AND SUPPLIES

1. Lots of scrap styrofoam
2. Toothpicks
3. Ice cream sticks
4. Wooden skewers

PROCEDURE

1. Put all the materials in an easy-to-reach area.
2. By putting sticks through the styrofoam, let the children create a million and one shapes and forms.
3. This could lead into a variety of storytelling activities.

MOLD A MÂCHÉ

MATERIALS AND SUPPLIES

1. Chicken wire
2. Newspaper
3. Prepared papier-mâché (the kind that can be mixed with water; it can be purchased at any hobby store)
4. Tempera paints
5. Brushes
6. Shellac

PROCEDURE

1. Create an animal shape out of chicken wire. This can be a real or an imaginary animal. Be sure to bend in all wire ends.
2. Have the children tear newspaper into 2-inch-wide strips. The length can vary up to 15 inches.
3. Prepare papier-mâché according to directions on package.
4. Dip the newspaper strips into the papier-mâché. Run your fingers across each strip to remove any excess.
5. Drape the wet strips over the wire form in a crisscross fashion. Be sure to overlap in all places.
6. Continue draping the newspaper until there are 3 or 4 layers.
7. Smooth out all the wrinkles and bumps with extra papier-mâché.
8. Let the form dry. This could take up to a week.
9. Use sandpaper to smooth the surface.
10. Use bright tempera paints to decorate your creation.
11. Allow to dry and add several coats of shellac.

TILE WORK

MATERIALS AND SUPPLIES

1. Bake-in-the-oven clay
2. Paint
3. Shellac
4. Wooden box
5. Epoxy glue

PROCEDURE

1. Give the children a theme to work around, such as the 4 seasons.
2. Roll out flat pieces of clay ¼ inch thick.
3. Cut the rolled clay into various shapes.
4. Give dimension to the tiles by adding shapes and textures.
5. When adding to a tile, slightly dampen it and then make crosshatchings with a fork or adhere new pieces.
6. Bake in the oven as the package directs.
7. Paint and shellac the finished tile.
8. Fasten to the box with glue.

BREAK A FACE

MATERIALS AND SUPPLIES

1. Chicken wire
2. Papier-mâché (the pre-mixed kind can be purchased at a hobby store)
3. Newspaper
4. Glue
5. Scissors
6. Tissue paper
7. Wrapped candy
8. Sandpaper
9. Tempera paint
10. Coat hanger

PROCEDURE

1. Make a simple round form out of the chicken wire. Leave a space large enough for 2 adult fists.
2. Straighten out the coat hanger and connect it to the top of the wire form.
3. Tear newspaper into 2-inch-wide strips, 10 to 15 inches long.
4. Prepare papier-mâché according to the package directions.
5. Dip the paper strips into the papier-mâché and remove any excess.
6. Stuff candy into the hole.
7. Drape the wet strips across the wire form in crisscross fashion. Cover the entire form, including the hole.
8. Put on 2 to 3 layers, making sure you cannot see the wire form.
9. Allow the form to dry. This could take up to a week.
10. When the form is dry, sand the rough edges.
11. Give the ball a primer coat of white to cover up the newsprint.
12. Paint a face on the form.

13. Hang hair made of tissue paper, and you've got a face you can break.
14. Use the coat hanger to suspend your piñata.
15. Blindfold each child and give him or her a bat to try to knock the candy out.
16. Be sure to keep all children out of the way of the swinging bat.

WOOD-WORKING

SUGGESTED NUMBER: 5 to 20

MATERIALS AND SUPPLIES

1. Hammers
2. Nails
3. Lots of scrap wood

PROCEDURE

1. Put out all the wood, nails, and hammers.
2. Ask the children to make something with the wood. Let them figure out what.
3. Sit back, cover your ears, have a few Band-Aids on hand, and enjoy the carpenters at work.

CARD HOUSE

SUGGESTED NUMBER: 2 to 10

MATERIALS AND SUPPLIES

1. Lots of playing cards
2. Lots of old greeting cards

PROCEDURE

1. Allow the children to build the biggest house they can with all the cards.
2. You might want to take pictures of these since they will not be permanent.

MOBILES

MATERIALS AND SUPPLIES

1. Wood dowels
2. Fishing line
3. Photograph of every child
4. Construction paper
5. Glue
6. Scissors

PROCEDURE

1. Give each child his or her picture, paper, glue, and scissors.
2. Have them make construction paper frames for their pictures.
3. With various lengths of string and dowels, construct a mobile using the pictures.

VARIATION

Use hand and foot prints.

TIE-DYEING

MATERIALS AND SUPPLIES

1. Large white piece of material or a sheet
2. Dye
3. Rubber bands
4. 2 buckets for each color

PROCEDURE

1. Give each child a handful of rubber bands. Twist the rubber bands around small pieces of material so they resemble little puffs.
2. Cover the sheet with the little puffs.
3. Put the entire sheet in the lightest dye (yellow, for example). Leave it in until it is a few shades darker than the desired color.
4. Ring out and put in cold water to set dye.
5. Remove half the rubber bands in various places on the sheet. White circles will be showing.
6. Replace the rubber bands in different spots on the sheet.
7. Prepare the next lightest dye (light green).
8. Dip the rubber band puffs in the dye, keeping them there until they are a few shades darker than the desired color.
9. Repeat steps 4 to 8.
10. Again ring out the sheet and rinse well.
11. Remove all the rubber bands and allow the sheet to dry out of direct sunlight.
12. Use for a wall-hanging or a room divider.

TRAINS

MATERIALS AND SUPPLIES

1. Various sizes of boxes
2. Scrap pieces of:
   aluminum foil
   yarn
   paper
   macaroni
   styrofoam boxes
   sequins
3. String

PROCEDURE

1. Let every child decorate a box in any way he or she chooses.
2. Tie the boxes together, 1 foot apart, with string.
3. Take turns pulling the train. Don't forget to make all the train noises!

TINKERTOYS

SUGGESTED NUMBER: 10 or more

MATERIALS AND SUPPLIES

Tinkertoys

134

1. Distribute the Tinkertoys to each member of the group—6 pieces per person.
2. Ask each member to make something.
3. Divide into small groups of 4 members or more.
4. Have each group make something that utilizes all parts.

WIRE SCULPTURE

SUGGESTED NUMBER: 6 or more

MATERIALS AND SUPPLIES

1. Different colors of tissue paper
2. 2-feet by 2-feet pieces of chicken wire

PROCEDURE

1. Divide into groups of 3.
2. Each group designs a picture or color scheme by putting tissue paper into chicken wire.
3. After each group finishes, the different projects can be hooked together.

PAPER-CUP CONSTRUC-TION

SUGGESTED NUMBER: 1 or more

MATERIALS AND SUPPLIES

1. Paper cups, all the same type and size
2. Paper clips, staples, or glue

PROCEDURE

1. Children paper clip or attach the cups together to form a design.
2. Children could work alone, but have them combine their individual projects into one large construction.
3. Wire the sculpture together for a collage.

CONVERSATION GAMES

6

ANIMAL HUNT

MATERIALS AND SUPPLIES

1. Hard candy
2. Blindfold

PROCEDURE

1. Divide into groups and assign each group a different animal (see Kid Sorting, p. 17).
2. Ask each group to practice its noise separately and then ask all the groups to make their noises at the same time.
3. Blindfold one member of the group.
4. All players get on their hands and knees.
5. The players move to a piece of candy and begin making their team noise. The blindfolded child is the only one that can pick up the candy. He or she must find his or her animal friends by listening and moving toward the noise.

ALPHABET SOUP

SUGGESTED NUMBER: 10 to 20

MATERIALS AND SUPPLIES

1. 10 copies of every letter of the alphabet
2. Construction paper
3. Glue
4. Scissors
5. Tape or pins

PROCEDURE

1. Ask each child to draw a soup bowl on a piece of construction paper.
2. Cut it out and tape or pin it to the child.
3. Give each child 6 letters.
4. By trading and bargaining with other children, each child tries to make his or her own name.
5. Glue the names on the soup bowls.

VARIATION

Appoint a banker and give him or her extra letters so that the children can bargain with the banker after they have exhausted their chances with the group.

COUNT AND SPELL YOUR FEET

SUGGESTED NUMBER: 5 or more

MATERIALS AND SUPPLIES

1. 4- by 6-inch sheets of paper or tag board that have been numbered consecutively, 1 digit per paper, or lettered, 1 letter per paper
2. Masking tape

PROCEDURE

1. With children seated on the floor, tape a numbered or lettered paper to the bottom of each foot.
2. If using numbers, call out numbers at random, and ask the children to show that number with their feet. Or, give them numbers to add or subtract, and ask them to give the answer with their feet.
3. If using letters, call out words to spell.
4. If there are enough children to divide into groups, give each group the letters of a word (the words having been chosen to make a sentence). After each group has formed its word, ask all groups to form themselves into a sentence.

VARIATIONS

1. Write numbers or letters on the children's feet with washable marking pens.
2. Try the game without talking.

FAMOUS FACES

MATERIALS AND SUPPLIES

1. Pictures of famous cartoon or TV characters
2. Tape

PROCEDURE

1. Tape a famous face on the back of every person playing.
2. The object is to find out who is on your back, but you need help. You may ask yes or no questions about your character to anyone in the group.
3. Continue asking and answering questions until you find out who is on your back.
4. The game is not over until everyone knows the name of the character taped on his or her back.
5. This game can be an end in itself, or it could be used to group the children for another activity. For example, use specific groups of characters—all those from "Peanuts," all those from "Sesame Street," and so on.

LEAD THE BLIND

SUGGESTED NUMBER: 2 or more

MATERIALS AND SUPPLIES

Blindfolds (1 per group)

PROCEDURE (see "Trust Walk," p. 145)

1. Blindfold 1 member of the team.
2. The blindfolded person can only be directed verbally.
3. Set up an obstacle course, such as crawling under a desk or table, sitting in a chair, going around a pole or any other object. Pick up an object that must be brought back to the group.
4. After each individual finishes the obstacle course, another member of the team tries. Continue until all children have had a turn.

TRUST WALK

SUGGESTED NUMBER: 2 or more

MATERIALS AND SUPPLIES

Blindfolds for each set of partners

PROCEDURE

1. The person not blindfolded takes the blindfolded partner on a walk, giving all instructions orally.
2. After 1 person has walked for a while, switch roles.

AUTOGRAPH

SUGGESTED NUMBER: 10 or more

MATERIALS AND SUPPLIES

1. A pencil for every child
2. A list of everyone in the group for each person present

PROCEDURE

1. Give each child a pencil and a list of all those present.
2. Ask each child to collect the signatures of all the others. Each person is to sign next to his or her name on the list.

CLASSMATE BINGO

MATERIALS AND SUPPLIES

1. A pencil for each child
2. On 8½- by 11-inch sheets of paper draw 25 boxes (5 across and 5 down) similar to a bingo card. Prepare 1 sheet for each child.
3. Write each child's full name on a 3- by 5-inch card.

PROCEDURE

1. Give each child a pencil and a sheet of boxed paper. Ask the children to write their own names in the center boxes.
2. Then each child goes to another, who puts his or her name in one of the boxes. Continue until all boxes are filled.
3. If there are not enough children to fill the 25 boxes, give them additional names to fill in anywhere they choose.
4. After this has been completed, play bingo with the cards by drawing the children's names and reading them.
5. Sheets can be switched or collected and saved for another day.

VARIATION

If the children are not acquainted with one another, have the child whose name is called to stand.

ODD-EVEN BEANS

SUGGESTED NUMBER: 10 or more

MATERIALS AND SUPPLIES

Bag of beans

PROCEDURE

1. Divide into teams.
2. Give each team an equal number of beans.
3. The team divides the beans in any manner the members wish.
4. The team members then separate and circulate around the room, offering a nonteam member the opportunity to guess whether they have an odd or even number of beans.
5. If the person guesses correctly, he or she gets the beans. If wrong, he or she gives up the number of beans in his or her hand.
6. Within a game, have different time limits, and allow the teams to regroup and redivide the beans among their team members.
7. Put a time limit on the entire game.

HIDDEN FACE

MATERIALS AND SUPPLIES

1. A number for each child
2. Paper sack for each child
3. Pencil and paper for each child
4. Masking tape

PROCEDURE

1. Pass out the above material. Have the children tape the numbers on their chests, cut 2 holes in the sacks for their eyes, and put the sacks over their heads.
2. The children walk around and write down the other children's numbers and the names they think correspond.
3. After a certain time limit, the children take off their sacks and check their answers.

VARIATIONS

1. With a large group, form teams. Put the even numbers on one team and the odd numbers on the other.
2. Use the same procedure as above except have the children write down only the number and names of nonteam members.
3. Have the teams combine their answers and form 1 complete list for the entire group.

PARTY LINE

SUGGESTED NUMBER: 7 or more

MATERIALS AND SUPPLIES: None

PROCEDURE

1. Seat the group in a circle.
2. Designate 1 child to whisper a thought or quote to the person on his or her left. That person then whispers what he or she heard to the next person.
3. The message continues around the circle. When it reaches the last person, he or she stands and announces the phrase.
4. The leader then tells the group what the original thought was.

VARIATION

Have 2 messages going in different directions.

I SPY

SUGGESTED NUMBER: 5 or more

MATERIALS AND SUPPLIES: None

PROCEDURE

1. One child starts the game by picking an object in the room and saying, "I spy with my little eyes something that is . . . ." He or she then gives the color or, for older children, the first letter of the item.
2. The other children try to guess the item.
3. The person who guesses leads the next game.

WHO AM I?

SUGGESTED NUMBER: 10 or more

MATERIALS AND SUPPLIES

A large blanket or sheet

PROCEDURE

1. Divide into 2 groups.
2. One group leaves the room and sends in a member, who is covered with a blanket.
3. This member crawls on the floor and occasionally snorts, groans, or makes a similar sound.
4. The members of the opposing group try to guess who is undercover, but they must agree as a group and give only 1 answer.
5. If they are correct, the opposing group must send in another player.
6. If they are incorrect, the groups change places, and the game continues.

AUNTIE GEN

SUGGESTED NUMBER: Groups of 5

MATERIALS AND SUPPLIES: None

PROCEDURE

1. Each group of 5 is seated in a circle.
2. One child is selected as a leader and opens the game by asking the person on his or her left, "Did you know my Auntie Gen?"
3. The person replies, "Which one of your aunts is that?" The leader replies, "The one that went like this."

150

4. The leader initiates an action, such as tapping his or her head with the right hand.
5. All members of the group imitate the leader.
6. The player on the leader's left then turns to the player on his or her left and asks (while tapping his head), "Did you know my Auntie Gen?"
7. The dialogue continues as before with this player adding an action.
8. The group imitates both actions simultaneously.
9. The idea is to see how many different actions can be done simultaneously.

CONVERSA-TION

SUGGESTED NUMBER: 2 or more

MATERIALS AND SUPPLIES

Bulletin board with numerous items pinned on it.

PROCEDURE

1. Let the group study the board for 1 minute.
2. The group then covers their eyes, and the leader removes one item.
3. The group opens their eyes and tries to guess which item is missing.
4. The game continues until most parts have been removed.

VARIATIONS

1. Play outdoors by placing objects on a blanket.
2. Instead of eliminating an item, add one. The group guesses which item has been added.

MY NAME BEGINS WITH

SUGGESTED NUMBER: 3 or more

MATERIALS AND SUPPLIES: None

PROCEDURE

1. Seat the children in a circle.
2. Ask each person to introduce himself or herself to everyone else.
3. Then each person stands up, says his or her name, and takes 1 minute to name everything in the room that starts with his or her first and last initials.

GROUP FORMS

SUGGESTED NUMBER: 10 or more

MATERIALS AND SUPPLIES: None

PROCEDURE

1. Ask the children to sit on the ground with their knees bent and their feet flat on the ground.
2. On a signal, the group forms the outline of a well-known object (for example, egg, triangle, circle, square, and so on).
3. The form should be closed, with each child able to lean on the child's knees behind him or her.
4. If group is large, divide into smaller groups and see who can form the best egg or triangle.